HEROES & KINGS

By CHARLES WILLIAMS
With Wood Engravings by
Norman Janes

the apocryphile press
BERKELEY, CA
www.apocryphile.org

Heroes and Kings was designed by Hubert J. Foss, and the wood engravings were made by Norman Janes. Three hundred copies, of which two hundred and fifty were for sale, were printed in the year 1930, on Barcham Green hand-made paper, in eighteen-point Monotype Caslon, by Henderson and Spalding Ltd., Sylvan Grove, Camberwell, London, S.E. 15

Apocryphile Press
1700 Shattuck Ave #81
Berkeley, CA 94709
www.apocryphile.org

ISBN 978-1-937002-20-6

Apocryphile edition, 2013. All rights reserved. Printed in the United States of America.

HEROES
& KINGS

Contents

BOAR'S HILL: 11 JULY 1929

For Robert Bridges

From a wise poet, and beauty loved and endured
  till beauty's self, obeying, now there awaits
  the bidding of mortal mind–from those holy gates
I issued, firmly of poetry's truth assured.
Oxford below, the hot sun above, abjured
  all tale but this—how 'mid his contending fates
  of darkness and cold man falters not but estates,
high-centered, all lovely words: then my heart, allured,
broke into prayer: *Me also awhile befriend,*
  O solitude, teacher of tongues; and thou, broad sky,
to whom man's life is shown, move thou the discreet
Muse, fair Contemplation, desirable friend,
  nor longer, for winter comes, let her deny
some verse to my mouth, of this hill not quite unmeet.

TO MICHAL:
ON HER HEARING MICE

In those past incarnations whence was drawn
   your holy and sweet spirit, being purged
of its first grossness there, and to the drawn
   of your to-day's perfection thence emerged,
what may you not have been–gipsy or thane,
   a cinquecento gem, an Indian squaw,
vizier of Delhi, squire Cambuscan,
   of some small flitting bunch of feather and
claw!
This you were not–the visionary mind
   who on a silent Babylonian roof
the earliest myth of Genesis designed,
   and of our Fall: for if you (take the proof)
had told that story—fatal to man's house—
the foe had been no serpent but a mouse.

ON KINGSHIP

For Humphrey Milford

That in the neighbourhood of mighty kings
  lives true delight for ever, this I knew
and tasted all the joy that order brings,
  headship, and ritual, when I looked on you,
Caesar, amid your officers last night;
  and more than you—the worth of majesty,
distinction, place, and courts in motion right
  around the Presence, so the king's head be
by the crown's self o'ershadowed; for the crown,
  not to be too much merited, lest man
suppose desert deserves it, shows his town
  not less, but more, O more, republican
when great equalities in order fall
and freedom's self grows hierarchical.

MICHAL, SAUL'S DAUGHTER

Which of thy lovers was thine equal, queen,
  twice Israel's royalty, whose fame bequeathed
  love meet for such great verse as later wreathed
Helen, thy sole compeer? thou, tossed between
the comely youth whom, when thine eyes had seen,
  thy heart desired, to whom thy quick lips breathed
  counsel of safety when the king's court seethed
with swords and plots; not known then for the mean
resentful tyrant who upon thy life
  avenged his own despite more than his god
   for that hot sneer *How glorious seemed the king:*
and him of Gallim who, in fear of strife,
  died not for love's sake at thy feet but trod
   only with tears after thy wayfaring.

JOHN STUART MILL AT AVIGNON

Within this second Rome the oracular See
  crowded its riches, liveried by France
o'er its own white and purple, to advance
the glory of that twin-born Majesty
whom the Pope lackeyed; where, ere Catherine's plea
  shook its device with sorrow, Petrarch's glance
  worshipped amid all rubied circumstance
a central pearl of loveliness; now he
whose lofty mind beholds the abstract line
  of intellectual argument and weighs
  the worth of each solemn irrefutable phrase,
moves, in devotion to a covered shrine;
  and the bright tumult on the magnificent hill
  wanes ghostlike from the colder dawn of Mill.

ON THE DEATH
OF THE QUEEN ALEXANDRA

When the queen-consorts of our English kings
    in a celestial lowlihood compare
their largest praise, and each in shyness brings
    some fragrant boast to light the heavenly air,
when one shall say: 'Forgive me Plantagenet
    starred England through with crosses'; one 'My word
brought Christ in', and so all in order set
are by their chosen hour of glory heard,
do not you speak of beauty or of grace,
    but let your single phrase of softness drop
into their union; utter from your place
    'Tennyson greeted me'—say that, and stop.
And all those queens shall wonder at your fame
royally laurelled with that lasting name.

THE HEPTAMERON

of Margaret, Queen of Navarre

Look, where the rich Renascence hath its end !
   Torches that smoked down the deep corridors
of Valois or of Bourbon now descend
   into small niches where the League, Cahors,
France and Guise falling, the Bartholomew,
   and love's most amorous and royal glee,
fade in a mirky twilight where some few
   clerks or poor shopmen sink uneasily
to the small dark, abominable shops,
   where, since deeds cannot be, they seek to frame
their dreams of deeds, the ragged curtain drops,
   but through some rent her still triumphant name
smites on the street in legended love from afar,
king's bride, king's sister–*Margaret of Navarre*.

FLINT CASTLE

Separate, upon a day,
earth and air and water lay.
Earth in ruined towers; the sky
arched and luminous on high;
and the river flowing near—
each a beauty did appear;
whose three lovelinesses made
a compacted whole, displayed
to the intellect and sight
in arrangement of delight.
Yet, by mortal judgement linked,
each from each lay still distinct;
none on other made advance
from its neighbouring romance;
ruined walls, unruined sky,
and the movement that went by,
picturesquely lay combined
for the pleasure of the mind.
Sudden, without wit or choice
of my will, began my voice:
The castle royally is manned,
my lord,—lo as the sudden scanned
syllables of verse unrolled,
all the vision grew ensouled;
from a borrowed castle spoke
Northumberland and Bolingbroke;

as the speech I did rehearse,
natural as the air to verse
grew the verse unto the air,
changing the horizon there,
the five accents half-divine
which are England's greatest gift
to the world from all her thrift
of empire, all her store of gold,
all her exploration bold,
all her victories and crowns,
all her seas and hills and downs—
none of these shall last so long
as the measure of her song;
till that verse of all took hold,
shaped them in its living mould,
and by soft unconscious power
changed the aspect of the hour.
Then the age-intinctured stone
and the azure arching zone
and the river flowing past,
all were one—were one at last.
Then the awful mind no more
was but what it was before,
a mere frame for knowledge; then
unity awoke again.
Walls and towers were 'ware thereof;
and the luminous sky above,
and the greensward underneath,

mingled in audible breath.
Through the eyes they inward passed,
and transfigured, on the vast
sound of verse re-issuing,
seemed within that verse to sing,
there to live, and there be true
to the Power that could indue
with its unity each one,
all their separations done.
By no memory renewed
of some outworn civil feud
round the broom where armoured men
trampled and clashed—it was not then
King Richard, no, nor Bolingbroke
who in plaintive pageant spoke;
there at most made time and space
for this verse to fill a place.
The castle gave to poetry
merely her naked chance to be,
but the child upon the chance
turned his o'erwhelming countenance,
and smiled to see how all things fell
under the utterance of his spell.

THE SONG OF THE DESERTED THRALL

My boy is in Jerusalem
   and all alone am I,
I cannot with the lassies talk
   that work so merrily
and kisses out of windows throw
   where their stout lads go by.

For round by the high capes of Spain
   and through the Roman Sea,
by Malta bays and Cyprus bays
   and ancient Sicily,
there sailed a ship to Jaffa town,
   and in that ship was he.

Tall Saracens and infidels
   there often he must meet,
and little vipers curling slide
   athwart the burning street,
while centipedes and scorpions dart
   their poison at his feet.

And when he finds Jerusalem
   and looks on Sheba's queen,
so prinked and decked and set about,
   so dainty is she seen,
as when she courted Suleiman,
   so washed and white and clean;

that he'll forget you, heavy feet,
   who have to trudge the mire,
and he'll forget you, dusty hands,
   who rake and make the fire,
and you, poor body, who have worn
   no soft or gay attire.

For when she sees him she will lose
   her dream of lovers gone,
and she will send her sixty kings
   to bring him to her throne,
and he shall rule Jerusalem
   and I shall die alone.

LILITH

The Majesty of Sheba, searching far
for lovelier forms of wisdom than of old
were taught her house by pre-diluvian kings,
and therefrom shining in herself more bright
than Helen on the landing-stage of Troy,
and braver in adornment than the Greek
by Antony in mid-Alexandrian throned,—
Balkis, in knowledge unsurpassed by him
before whose coming there palace where she stood
hushed itself, falling prostrate, saw the king
stand in the portal, vestmented and crowned,
Solomon.
    Upright a moment ere she sank
earthward with all his powers of earth and air,
ambassadors from China and from Crete,
lords of the law, chieftains, and genii,
she lingered from obeiasance, and alone
over the prostrate turbans, helms, and crowns,
the eyes of Sheba communed with the king.

Then in silence Solomon throned himself.
and visibly of a sudden above the chair
hung the four Angels, at each corner one,—
a pillar of turning dust; and vanishing rain;
flicker of fire; and brightness of moving air—
manifest measurements of the universe,
elements and ideas of the changing world:
Beneath, low couched the lions—material strength

leashed to the will of its lord: Jerusalem
reposed in the king's justice; only at hand
were heard the toilers in the Temple courts
who ceased not night or morning, and far off
came from the Syrian deserts a thousand leagues
the thin tormented call of Iblis: 'Think,
Commander of the Faithful, think on hell'.

Then the hall breathed and rose and knelt and rose;
Sheba, with downcast look and doubtful hand
touching the sceptre, felt upon her face
Solomon's heavy luminous eyes, and sat,
enthroned a step below him but a hand,
beholding while each cause before the king
was brought for judgement,—nations, peoples, lords,
and children; for the king's word went abroad
bidding no tenderest trouble brood unjudged
if the need of the Glory of God might make it whole:
Wherefore the guard stood spearless by the door
and the land's learnings gravely sat to hear
while the king healed the anguish of the young.

But when that day's last summons was to sound,
a final trumpet blowing o'er the world
lest aught of justice rest unsatisfied,
forth from the doctors on the king's right hand
an old man, wise in the writ and the unwrit law,
stole to the throne's foot, sighing: 'Viceregent of God,
forty years since, they servant on a night
wrought mischievously, but thereafter turned
with tears and lamentation and penitence

till the repose of God another night
woke in my breast: saying "It is forgiven; sleep".
Is not all well?'
                    The king said: 'All is well.
What seekest thou?'
                                'Night by night, every night,
for forty years of night,' the other said,
'comes, in that moment when the deed was done,
a foul thing out of the Pit and lies with me
for a full hour's space. Commander of devils, cause
Hell's gates to lock: Viceregent of God, proclaim
God's word in the nethermost. Shall the Eternal mock
at His own pardon? but only for thy fame
perchance so long He leaves the abyss unsealed.'

Then the king lifted up his hand, whereon,
within the single stone that was the ring,
moved, flamelike interwoven, uttering song,
the four intelligible letters, whose core—
and blinded fell the hall—one speck of light,
incredibly remote, incredibly pure,
was but so much of the Shekinah's self
as Solomon's might bear to view undazed:
and the king cried and said: 'Deceiver of man,
Lilith, depart and trouble the world no more!'
Then to his suppliant: 'Of two judgements one,
as thou hast prayed or hast not: thine to choose—
freedom and peace and slumber, since the worlds
obey me, and all the Jinn; but think that so
thou, crying aloud for pardon, hast but sought
thine own rest, thine own quietude—not God;

or this thy visitation till the end
and to know thou willest naught but only God:
Choose.'

        The man answered slowly, veiling his face:
'Amen; I take refuge with God.'

              And the king said:
'The Lord thy God be with thee: go in peace.'

Even on the word from the crowd beyond the hall
one rushed, distraught, impetuous; at the throne
cast himself down, and cried: 'Hear, hear, O king,
do justice, render me my own, destroy
the insolent breacher of God's law and thine!
In the name of the Undeceiving, do me right!
Thy servant loved a man, heart to his heart,
as my lord's father loved Prince Jonathan.
In meditation, in discourse, in act,
our ways ran level; no another love
fractured in its youth, nor in its age our wives
fingered our friendship roughly. O avenge!
I in my traffic being bound forth to Tyre
left in his charge my store, my strength, my gold;
and now returned, lo is nor friend nor gold:
He hath betrayed our love, his guile hath robbed
my all of future peace out of my hand,
thriving thereon at Thebes. My name is dirt;
men mock me, men besmear me. Wisdom, judge:
send me a squadron and restore my right,
my gold, my years' provision, and for him,
let the king's world be on him till he die!'

He ceased, and the king said: 'Hast thou kept faith
in all things with him? hast thou wholly loved?'

The man said: 'By thy father's head I swear
the love I knew in him was love in God.'

Then the king lifted his hand again, and cried
till the hall shook: 'Deceiver of Adam, depart!
O Mother of Iblis, trouble the man no more!'
Then to his suppliant: 'Of two judgements, one,
as thou hast loved or hast not—thine to choose:
Either a squadron, pursuit, and in thy hands
they friend laid fettered and thy riches free,
but therein the knowledge thou hast never loved;
or else no satisfaction till the end
but that thy past indeed was his and love's.
Choose.'
            And the man covered his face and sighed:
'Amen: I loved and love.'
                              And the king said:
'The Lord thy God be with thee: go in peace.'

Then cried the trumpets and the Divan closed.

But when at eve the seeker of heavenly things,
Balkis the queen, with Solomon lay at meat,
his vestments and his crown being put aside
in the king's treasury, and the Ring itself
casketed in his secret oratory,
after high talk of how to shape a land,
of armies, when to war and how to make peace,
of agriculture and the tents made huts,

the queen a little paused, smiling, and said:
'Viceregent of God, may the least of thy servants learn
of these things that were done to-day?' And he:
'Is not my will made wholly one with thine?
Ask.'

And she said: 'When my lord lifted up
his hand? and the words that my lord cried in the hall?
and the judgements given?'

The king said: 'Hear me tale:
in the beginning it is written thus—

'Adam our origin, yet wholly one,
nor right and left disparted into sex
or other means of love, in Eden lay
sleeping, and all the world that wakes by night
rejoiced around them, nor by night or day
was Paradise by uttered happiness
uncheered, nor died the song at even or morn,
whether the lions or the elephants
massed themselves, or with all else were subdued
to one bee's hum vibrating thanks to God:
but on this night o'er one large ankle slid
a little snake; our lord the Adam woke
in giant majesty, nor then again
slept, but in very ease of being rose
and, lightly lost in wonder at themselves,
moved through the moon-dazed garden; in the paths
before them ran the winged child Memory,
not yet a consolation or a curse,
but mere delight of knowledge, added joy,
who through the heights and depths of Paradise

led forth Adam, till at last they came
to the extreme land's border and beheld
the full Euphrates; at their feet beheld
a fringe of the delta of the river of life,
Euphrates, the least mouth of all the mouths
wherein the eternal waters from their cave
plunge throughout the visibility and time
to an unknown and unimagined end,
and interflow creation, on their waves
bearing the whole sidereal universe
with all its fellows, glancing here and there

on mortal sight in Ganges, Tiber, Nile,
or little pools, or mountain-falls, or seas,
or that same river, darkened now from joy,
Euphrates of the desert and the towns.

'Thither the Adam came, drunk with themselves,
so large in frame, so strong a lord they seemed
over the garden, by earth adored,
the very head and consciousness of life,
alone in mystery, alone in pride;
all things they understood, but not themselves
nor that they imaged; the Desire that flowed
before them rippled at their feet and shone,
the floating mirror of the floating moon,
a dim enchantment, where the Adam saw
their image and adored, blessed it and said:
"Wonderful art thou, man, within thy world!
O our desire, O beauty of all love,
for this we create ourselves, this hour
did we in our eternity conceive!
O cool reflection, O fair dream, O sweet
mystery of our own face beheld and loved,
thou softer than ourself, more pliable
than any dreamed perfectedness of law,
thou chief of Paradise, from this same hour
be there divorce 'twixt us and all but thee—
thou being ourself, ourself our only love."

'But on the farther side of the river stood
in a sterile land, unseen, impalpable,
he who was once a god, the Adversary,

fallen Demiurgis, blackened Lucifer,
stretched towards the river his pale magical hands,
and cried to it: "Be fruitful, multiply!
Hear your lord's word, O river, and bring forth
wraiths, and dim mockeries of desire and fear!
Come, goblins, dreams, miasmas, incubi,
fables, illusions, phantasms! wreathe his head,
blind him, and be with him by night and day,
his sole possession; and you chief arise,
Lilith, my own loved mother, my sole friend,
sole fruit of all unfruitful things, arise!
Vapour of all creation, whom not God
creating can forbid, be o'er man's world
thick vapour; as his word was, so fulfil
his Eden and his day! Blindness, awake!
In all his councils and conspiracies
deceive him with himself; in all his paths
of amorous hope, pious austerity,
draw him to adoration of himself;
O thou that art not, hide the things that are!"

'She heard, she rose; Lilith, who guile in heaven
first drenched the morning star, heard her son's call,—
the image of Adam in the stream
flowed up dilating, and took shape and hung,
now Adam, now herself, impalpable,
sterile, confusion and calamity,
and stole betwixt Euphrates and the moon,
and climbing as a mist about the land
in goblins, dreams, illusions, incubi,

dispersed herself; who, when the Adam turned
rejoicing into Eden, after them
in flakes and whorls and streamers drifted far
over the garden, hiding the rich lands
and thickly in the centre gathering fast
till the great trunks of the Trees of Knowledge and Life
were hid, nor aught but intertangled maze
of twining branches thinly showed themselves
and none knew of which tree which twig was sprung.
Thus Lilith came, thus the Deceiver flowed
o'er Paradise; dimly the Adam went
with dreaming mind and wandering steps, nor knew
themselves for truth nor Paradise nor God,
of all oblivious but oblivion.

'This the Unnameable saw, and to his sons
imparting said: "Which of you, O ye gods,
hath light within himself to part the cloud?
Whose star shall burn for guide? Who shall be known
to man for other than himself? Ye heavens,
that lucid to each other burn and shine,
which of you all shall be to man again
wonder and joy and truth and shining love?"
But Michael answered, mightiest of the gods,
"Hath not the chief of heaven, the Morning Star,
from his just path plunged in that mist to doom?
O fount of Lilith, Lilith none but thou
canst lighten, in whose mist our fiery sword
burns dim, and helpless wanders heavenly war."
To whom the Eternal: "Wisely have ye said,
children; nor good nor jinn nor man but We
shall be to man the self whom he adores,
when the appointed time bring forth the hour.
Now therefore since himself alone he knows,
let difference which is We; adore and know
what stroke within him prophesies of Us."

'Then as the Adam fell again to sleep
with separating finger God first clove
man's heart with hunger for the heart of man,
and brought forth Eve; in Eve all times that know
division, in division all surprise,
humility, and knowledge, all that once
brought Babel to disaster, that great town
which Nimrod at the spell of Lilith wrought
to show himself the god he dreamed he was.

'She therefore, man's beholden self, went forth
from Adam her compeer; she in the mist
deceived anew of Lilith but not slain,
nor robbed of her conceptions, from whose womb
issue all loves of friend or wife or child,
whom no man loves, no friend nor wife nor child,
but them the single ray of light divides,
making division wonder; and therein
a unity of wonder, job, and love—
love whom to know is the chief end of man.
Marvel not therefore if the engraven name
shed light in Lilith, nor if these to-day
bore not to see themselves phantasmally
err from the single and strait path of love
made absolute within himself, austere,
implacable, intelligible, one.'

But the queen answered: 'O Viceregent of God,
is love division? is division the end?
Instruct me, O wise king, how grows the joy
but by division after unity?'

'O perfect one,' the king said, 'for such cause
the Eternal shaped a woman and no man
out of the sleeping Adam, that his flesh,
more than the drowsy and deceiving mind,
might know amidst the illusions of content
heart-rending union; and thereafter comes
heart-healing separation.'

The queen said:
'Hath this face also somewhere, at some time,
out of some heart dispelled the Mother of Grief?
O master of Israel, tell me, dost thou know?'
But Solomon bowed himself to her and said:
'O Balkis, fairest of women, daughter of Eve,
though the Shekinah—be its name adored!—
lighten from this my office o'er the world
and make the Divan one lucidity,
was there lucidity within my heart?
Though my voice be to all the enchanted world
Bath Kol, the Daughter of the Voice, what sound
was heard within me? O thou second Eve,
O thou lucidity, O thou new voice,
what joy more swiftly from deception runs
before us now than that the Eternal meant
when from a trance he made her?'
                              The queen said
softly: 'Behold the handmaid of my lord'.

THE SINGING FISH

For Michael, who supplied the first two lines

The singing fish has golden eyes,
  has golden eyes that look so wild,
and a scaled body shaped with thighs,
  and utterance jubilant and mild.

Whether 'tis one of us that swims,
  a prince by old enchantment changed
and sent to float where water dims
  the eyes that once the mountains ranged;

whether he did Poseidon hail,
  an augur of the aqueous mind,
interpreting to shrimp and whale
  godhead erratically kind;

of whether him the fisher caught
  whom in return for rough goodwill
he blessed with riches passing thought—
  hut, manor, castle, palace—till

the greedy wife's incessant prayer
  turned blessing backward into bane
and brought on them the ancient care
  of struggling poverty again;

or of some prediluvian shoal
  ere man and fish had grown apart
this singing champion kept a soul
  and throve by half a human heart,

and, time-untouched and net-unsnared,
  grew mightier and more tuneful so,
and through the centuries largely fared,
  we know not—only this we know :

the singing fish has golden eyes,
  has golden eyes that look so wild,
and a scaled body shaped with thighs,
  and utterance jubilant and mild.

JIM CROW

Seven maids all wanting rings,
  jump, Jim Crow,
gold and pearls and jewels in them.
  Jump, Jim Crow!
Jim Crow is the latest of a very ancient line,
his only food is biscuits and his only drink is wine,
and seven butlers wait on him when he sits down to dine.
  Jump, Jim Crow! Jump, Jim Crow.

Seven maids all in a field,
  jump, Jim Crow,
all a-chatting in a field,
  jump, Jim Crow!
They saw Jim Crow come walking by; his dress was monstrous fine
his waving plumes were two feet five; his sword was two foot nine;
his cloak and doublet were of silk, of elegant design.
  Jump, Jim Crow! jump, Jim Crow!

'What to serve you can I do?
  Jump, Jim Crow!
Of gold or lands are you in need?'
  Jump, Jim Crow!
'Neither gold nor lands we need but each a husband strong;
to lend an arm and lend a smile and help a maid along,
within his pouch a crust of bread, within his mouth a song.'
  Jump, Jim Crow! Jump, Jim Crow!

'Seven butlers serve my chair,
  jump, Jim Crow,

all a-sighing all the day,
  jump, Jim Crow!
For seven maids they saw afar when light began to sink;
so lonelily, so cloudily, so wonderingly they think,
they bring me only scones to eat and lemonade to drink.'
  Jump, Jim Crow! Jump, Jim Crow!

All the maids began to cry:
  jump, Jim Crow,
'I will not wed a serving man:
  jump, Jim Crow!
For who am I'—'and who am I'—'and who am I'—'and I
to wait upon a master's chair and serve a mistress' eye,
and run to pick the children up and soothe them when they
cry?'
  Jump, Jim Crow! Jump, Jim Crow!

'One of them is a king's son;
  jump, Jim Crow,

and one is a sea-captain's boy,
  jump, Jim Crow,
and he has trod his father's deck and sailed around Cape Horn;
and one's a London citizen; and two are gentlemen born;
and two are jolly country lads with many fields of corn.'
  Jump, Jim Crow! Jump, Jim Crow!

'If one of them's a farmer's son,
  jump, Jim Crow,
I am his,' said Dorothy,
  jump, Jim Crow,
'Early will I rise with him before the dawn's begun,
and have his supper laid at night when all his work is done,
and see the fields all growing green and join the harvest fun.'
  Jump, Jim Crow! Jump, Jim Crow!

'If another is a farmer's son,
  jump, Jim Crow,
I will wed him,' said Suzanne,
  jump, Jim Crow,
'to know the queen bees hiving, and the horses trotting by,
the sheep in fold, the cows in shed, the sucking-pig in sty,
and the great bull in the meadow with his little angry eye.'
  Jump, Jim Crow! Jump, Jim Crow!

'If one of them's a gentleman born,
  jump, Jim Crow,
I am his,' said Rosalind,
  jump, Jim Crow,
'to see the Hunt and walk the lawn and ride out everywhere,

and once a year to go with him, so curled and gay and fair,
and see him in the Parliament below the Speaker's chair.'
    Jump, Jim Crow! Jump, Jim Crow!

'If another gentleman,
    jump, Jim Crow,
I am his,' Lucilla said,
    jump, Jim Crow,
'to read within the galleries of all his knightly race
'mid cabinets of porcelain and miniatures and lace
 such verse of lordly poets as is lovelier than my face.'
    Jump, Jim Crow! Jump, Jim Crow!

'If one of them's a sailor lad,
    jump, Jim Crow,
I will sail with him,' said Joan,
    jump, Jim Crow,
'to hear the sailor's chanty and to join the sailor's song,
to see Colombo and Cape Horn, Vesuvius and Hong Kong,
and to keep the quarter-deck with him when mutineers are strong.'
    Jump, Jim Crow! Jump, Jim Crow!

'If one of them's a London man,
    jump, Jim Crow,
I am his,' said Margaret,
    jump, Jim Crow,
'for I was born and I was bred in a tall house of Cheapside,
and to be wed in London town it shall be much my pride,
in Saint Andrew by the Wardrobe or Saint Olave or Saint Bride.'
    Jump, Jim Crow! Jump, Jim Crow!

'If one of them is a king's son,
  jump, Jim Crow,
I will marry him,' said Denise,
  jump, Jim Crow!
'My nurse who was a wise-woman has told me ages since
that I should walk in cloth gold and marry a royal prince
and live in a house of smooth marble with a wall of angry flints.'
  Jump, Jim Crow! Jump, Jim Crow!

Jim Crow gave the wedding feast,
  jump, Jim Crow!
Manors seven he offered them,
  jump, Jim Crow!
But the king's son in a month conveyed his bride away,
and in a week the captain's son took ship within the bay,
but the London man and London maid rode forth that very day.
  Jump, Jim Crow! Jump, Jim Crow!

TRISTRAM'S SONG TO ISEULT

The lord Tristram of Lyonesse, being fled with Iseult
from Tintagel in a refuge of woods, makes a poem
for her on the last night of their repose, and then
sings of its proper inditing.

Above all songs of Roman dames long dead
   I have made a song to bid thine image live.
Iseult; now therefore ere the night be sped,
   bid me fulfil the work I gave to give:
for I am Tristram, I have toiled for thee:
thou, now shalt thou my precious vellum be.
   Wear my new song, O thou my song enclosed,
for mine, its maker's glory, till the day
   redden the rose-rhymes thou hast still ourosed,
and thy poor singer is become a stray
(The dawn must come and I be ridden away!).

Who on this night of all the Table wakes
   to worship and to such protracted glee?
For there in Camelot the Archbishop flakes
   their roofs and eaves with white austerity;
and if the Queen and Lancelot find their joy
are they not chambered in the world's annoy,
   where Agravaine about the keyhole spies?
but in the woods and spring forbids the snow
   and in the woods there are no watching eyes
to overpeer our wealth of pretty show

(The stream is running; thou too soon must go).

Uncover ceremonially, O yet
  with an intense unceremonious mirth
make laughter of the wisdom on thee set,
  and be more gleeful of thine own fair earth.
Audaciously thy sweet behaviour frame
to make more flagrant the uprushing shame;
  set off thy blazon with true heraldry,
gules to its or—devisal not delay!
  come to this mode of worship worshipfully;
thus art thou purely mortal, and no fay
(The dawn must come and I be ridden away!).

Come, for the candles from their sockets shine,
  the logs burn clear, the world is far away;
come, yield thyself now to this clear design
  I draw upon thee, as on rougher clay
Athenian potters drew the images
of Zeus and all Olympian deities,
  till on thyself such ornaments thou display
as would make Pallas envious, did she know,
  or Aphrodite, who long Paphian day
scarce found such dear device of light and glow
(The stream is running; thou too soon must go).

Sink on this boar's skin, and on either side
  let the supporting arms and pedestalled hands
be as a living frame, where, rayed and eyed,
  the soft-chased vessel of thy spirit stands.

Be still, lift up thy face, and let me now
shape on the single and most luminous brow
    that title where to other lands and times
shall be discovered this excelling play
    of love's delight, and how with the sudden rhymes
women shall blush as May-trees with their May
(The dawn must come and I be ridden away!).

Iseult! and be that face no further marred
    by any writing; here, between the breasts,
be the magnificent opening slowly starred
    till it with new significance invests—
if that might be—those double summits fair;
and let the full stream issue forth from there,
    as Ganges from Mount Meru plunges free,
while delicate girdles round their bases grow;
    then let it draw, again a unity,

to new divorce, a stanza's length below
(The stream is running; thou too soon must go).

Bestow thyself upon my carriage! back!
    now sink into prostration; now the work
subtly discovers a more narrow track
    of difficult art; nor let this cunning irk
thy patience, while around the columned thighs
in diligence descent the quick brush plies,
    and curves in following spirals, as the Turk
the Ka'abah circumambulates, sent to pray
    by lying prophets; as in that stone lurk
false glamours, here true lights themselves array
(The dawn must come and I be ridden away!).

Round calves and ankles draws a golden chain,
    around the very parts it glorifies!
Now, for the culmination of the strain,
    turn to obscurity those happy eyes:
to arms and shoulders stanzas we allot;
the mid spine hath the penultimate; the knot
    and envoy at the very bottom lies.
There the proud syllables, marvellous and slow,
    utter themselves, never in prouder guise,
and all my manuscript is ended so
(The stream is running; thou too soon must go).

Iseult! Iseult! Rise, princess, and behold!
    thy mirror; view my large engraver's art!
Thou art of song and it of thee the mould;

either in either hath a proper part!
Call now on Mark, and bid him come and see
the woven piece that I have wrought for thee!
   Was any raiment like to this before?
which in thy cupboards no old nurse can lay,
   nor slurred, could Queen's tirewomen restore
though Cornwall's diadem were given in pay
(The dawn must come and I be ridden away!).

Here let each lover's burdened heart find easer
   in understanding of his ravishment;
since in his horoscope of mysteries
   each palpitation is with meaning blent!
Inscribed upon the harp is now the chart
of all the very music that thou art;
   look, what wise illustration from the lore
of deep antiquity bedecks thee so,
   brought in Greek simile, Roman metaphor,
and Asian incantations sorcerers know
(The stream is running; thou too soon must go).

Lo! my new-plotted, new-stained arms of love!
   for now my mistress is become my squire,
and her whole house, with all the parts thereof,
   cries *Tristram* which each breath she doth respire,
so brightly with my militant coat indued,
with mottoes and devices interstrewed
   more than great Arthur's crown imperial
can mean or Taliessin's art can cay;

it is my trumpet and it is my call
which here my infinite vassal doth obey
(The dawn must come and I be ridden away!).

The stream is running; thou too soon must go.
  The glorious work is ended; now undo,
 undo, Iseult, the detail of the show;
  put on the clearness thou art native to.
For I am Tristram; I have made this sight
lovely to us and lovely to the night,
  O song, O my great song, O proud and gay!
Champions shall honour there but never so:
  The dawn is come, I must be ridden away—
cease to behold it then and cease to know:
  The stream is running; thou too soon must go.

PALOMIDES' SONG OF ISEULT

The lord Palomides the Saracen, being denied and mocked by queen Iseult, makes a song of the hope-lessness of love.

Now have I no more care
to follow the Blatant Beast
for the sake of Iseult the Fair;
from all but the making of rhymes
have I, Palomides, ceased
in these disastrous times.

And even the poor rhymes say,
as the wind blows them down,
'Though we bring peace to-day,
to-morrow you shall destroy
our music with a sad frown,
since there is no more joy'.

Go then, complain where ye choose
saying I use you ill;
saying I must refuse
the songs that used to thrive;
because I have no more will
after my death to live.

You have lived long enough, rhymes,
when you have saddened me more,

prolonging disastrous times;
you are not as those that came
in months now nearly a score,
rushing in wind and flame.

Singing shall pass, and you,
rhymes, certes you must die;
death is your promised due.
If I minded you it would seem
I held you worthy to lie
next to a wounded dream.

There is nothing I know,
which is worthy to be the myrrh
wherewith, embalming so
the image of my rest
an building its sepulchre,
I banish her from my breast.

But all things that I have
I will bring, as of old men brought
to the mouth of a kingly grave
riches, and there in the gloom,
following a deathly thought,
made a great hecatomb.

I will bring them, as the herds,
the flocks, the slaves, the wives,
the jewels, the palace-birds,
and over a bloody year
I will pour out all my lives,
only to bury her here.

All weapons, all essays
towards song and chivalry,
all longing for great affrays,
all princely neighbourhood,
all rites, all bending the knee,
all glory of ill or good,

all quest, all knowledge, all hope,
all longing for delight,
all, all shall have their scope
cut short, and perish from the earth,
going down into night;
for there is no more worth.

Now if she rise no more,
nothing at all shall rise;

my soul as a mother bore
children, that shall not abound,
but when their few days are o'er
be sacrificed to Mahound.

For the rulers of old are here,
lowering over me;
no more I fight them or fear;
perpetually sacrificed
I resist not their deity
since she was one with Christ.

Happy be she and praised,
honoured be she and sung,
blessed be she and raised
to the house where the princes are,
speaking the proper tongue
that is known in the Morning Star;

but you, my rhymes, shall die,
be you now but a pall
over a corpse borne by
where, when to-day is gone,
Palomides (she will not recall)
sang that my forehead shone.

LAMORACK'S SONG TO MORGAUSE

The lord Lamoracke de Galis, being in a castle with the queen Morgause, King Lot's wife and King Arthur's sister, makes a song of the joy and grief that come by her.

I Lamoracke have bound to-day
the queen my mistress in our play.
   Though she contended, with white hands,
I have driven her courage into flight
   and made her body fast with bands,
doing her arrogance despite,
till the queen, till the queen was fain
to pray to be released again;
I have bound her for cause and for no cause,
the queen of Orkney, the queen Morgause!

In a turret chamber of my hold
I have a bed of beaten gold,
   brought from a Moorish tower in Spain,
with cushions and rich tapestries
   for the rest and cover overlain,
whereon I oft have taken ease;
but there to-day I cast her down
without a robe, without a crown,
bound and prisoned for love's good laws,
the queen of Orkney, the queen Morgause!

—49—

Under the Fate that threatened us,
in days that are heavy and ruinous,
   we have made a little lovely hour;
we have forgot the prophecies,
   smiling to feel the joyous power
and the glee and the gay felicities
which were between us manifest
till we broke to battle and broke to rest,
and love was quickened with love's applause
O the queen of Orkney, the queen Morgause!

This could I not devise, but lo
even on a sudden it is so;
   see, I have sealed it with a kiss.
I kissed my vassal as I would—
   O freedom that this bondage is!
how hath she entered into good,
though high she thwarted all attack,
yea, nigh she conquered Lamoracke,
but I bound her for a gracious cause,
the queen of Orkney, the queen Morgause.

But the queen's majesty was strong
and kept her battle overlong:
   she fled not from the first alarm,
she broke wrists out of my grasp,
   my hand she wrested from her arm,
and her lithe body from my clasp—
behold, her potency was past,

ankles and wrists were corded fast.
I made her the victim or Love's laws,
the queen of Orkney, the queen Morgause!

Her shoulder that pushed hard at me
I brought into captivity;
   yea, yet it ached from a harsh hand,
with all her clear embattled side.

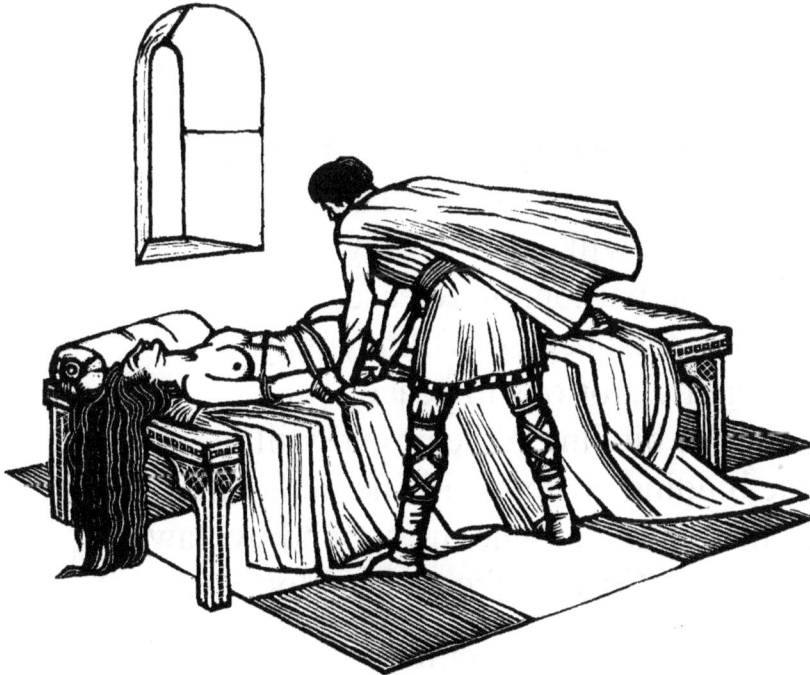

   Her feet that did so firmly stand
had power of movement quite denied;
she who in combat was so firm
was brought unto a helpless term;
I bound her for cause and for no cause,
the queen of Orkney, the queen Morgause!

But when her strife was broken at last
in silken ropes I made her fast
  and laid her on a golden bed.
Then being drunk with sight of love
  and vision of her prostrate head
I bade my harpstrings cry and move.
I saw a greater binding come,
and the queen lying still and dumb
for Logres' agony and its cause—
the queen of Orkney, the queen Morgause!

My hands to the harp for terror sprang,
for anguish and pity of love I sang:
  'Is there no will, is there no way,
no grace, no pardon, no release,
  whereby the queen of Orkney may
be brought victorious to peace,
save by the binding of heart and will,
by the binding of limbs till she lieth still,
from the night that whelms her and overawes
the queen of Orkney, the queen Morgause?

'O beauty fairer than Iseult
when Love for marriage struck his bolt
  through both Lord Tristram's heart and hers
in an hour of sun on the Irish Sea!
  O majesty greater than Guinevere's
when she sits enthroned at the King's tournèy,
and moans for Lord Lancelot there below,

seeing Love's spear bent to his overthrow,
as here, on a hurdle and bound, Love draws
the queen of Orkney, the queen Morgause!

'For when the frenzies of love awoke
in Balin's wrath and Dolorous Stroke,
   and darkness fell on the earth
and mischief drew upon Camelot,
   then all fair things that had one birth
their amity and love forgot,
and wounded was the Hidden Crown,
and Balin smote his brother down,
and the mother of dragons struck her claws
in the queen of Orkney, the queen Morgause!

'Knowledge of kinship wholly died
and the track of the Blatant Beast ran wide,
   because of the hurt that Balin did
when he caught to himself the Holy Thing
   and wrought upon earth a deed forbid,
and wounded the side of the Guardian King:
then Arthur knew not a hidden face
but caught his sister to his embrace;
kinship and kingship were broken laws—
O the queen of Orkney, the queen Morgause!

'For Arthur's sister, the queen Morgause,
being fashioned without any flaws,
   fair without and fair within,
body and soul most wondrous fair,

came on a night to a dark inn,
and found a stranger ridden there,
whom for his hardihood and grace
she let prevail on her embrace,
and the start wheeled and Death made pause
o'er the queen of Orkney, the queen Morgause!

'Out of that hour came bitter dearth
for Mordred, the king's band, had birth,
   and still with malice in his breath
points hand and tongue at the Table Round;
   he in great venom skirmisheth
wherever glorious fates abound:
Now am I come to her full late
to be of help to her estate;
sad is she grown for an evil cause,
the queen of Orkney, the queen Morgause!

'Vain is it now to curse or pray;
yea, now there is but one thing to say—
   lie low, my queen, and hear it said,
lie white and still and hear it sung
   over that silent prostrate head—
though the prayer have failed and the curse have clung,
I cry, as the doom works out its end,
"I am Lamoracke in her cause,
the queen of Orkney, the queen Morgause!"

'When thou art walking and gazing forth
out of thy castle in the north,

and King Lot looketh askance at thee;
when thou art sitting in thy stall
   amid the horns of courteous glee,
and the queens and the kings in Arthur's hall—
   when thou seest the shadow upon Iseult
and round Guinevere the swords revolt,
remember me and the love that draws,
O queen of Orkney, O queen Morgause!

'When thou art bound in a direful fate
and the world around thee is desolate,
   remember this hour, remember well,
in the crashing of Orkney and Camelot,
   how we took this joy ere the great doom fell,
and were glad awhile, and awhile forgot;
how while thou layest fast bound in a thong,
I Lamoracke made and chanted a song,
how I bound there for cause, and for no cause,
the queen of Orkney, the queen Morgause!

'Yea then thou shalt be in the end set free,
even now as I kneel to unfasten thee,
   yea, now as thine arms go round my neck,
yea, now as thou leapest to my embrace,
   will I come to thee in the midst of wreck,
I will set my spear at thy foeman's face,
I will ride and cry, as the kingdoms end,
"I am Lamoracke and her friend,
Lamorake, Lamoracke, in her cause,
the queen of Orkney, the queen Morgause!"'

PERCIVALE'S SONG TO
BLANCHFLEUR

*The lord Percivale de Galis, coming to the Maiden
Castle, is asked by Blanchfleur his sister in sanctity
concerning the Chivalry of the Table, and makes
answer.*

In the Name of the Invisible Unity
by whom are all things, and in all is He.

This to record, beyond all myths, the myth
of Britain and they body one therewith;
for coming on this night, sister, I saw
astonished and adoring and in awe,
how the tale means but thee and thou the tale,
and after what dark manner the dark grail
is manifested and mistaken not
through a shape fairer than was Camelot.

O happy asking now, that bids me brood
over that Chivalry, and for neighbourhood
lends those clear slender fingers through whose glass
I have seen the lordship of the Table pass;
which, honouring still in timeless time, I name
now first aright, and o'er them all proclaim
their titles—touch with one each delicate back
after my will: mid-right, Sir Lamoracke;

next to him, Sir Bedivere; next him, Sir Kay
(the smallest he, as least a knight they say);
Sir Mador de la Porte; Sir Agravaine,
nearest his brother: mid-left Sir Gawaine;
Sir Gareth des Beaux Mains; Sir Gaheris;
Sir Dinadan; Sir Persant of Inde—and this
leads me to each twin state of strife and calm,
each comfortable and most sacred palm,
wherein the grace of holy Order lies,
who are the bishops in their panoplies
of Winchester and Canterbury: yea,
princess, if any kiss them any day,
bid him remember, after his own mode,
why shy reserve of sanctity in them showed.

Ha, but I linger no more on those fair
honourable priesthoods, those most cool and rare
centres of consecrating energy;
let pass to where must needs lie more of thee—
finding along the royalties of thine arms
(allied with Camelot, and by false alarms
ever unstirred, open to love alone,
where undesirous love can be made known),
King Bagdemagus and King Pellinore,
King Lot, King Ban—lo, where a richer store
of royalty, chivalry, and of beauty flows,
and thy deep student a deep secret knows.
See, see, thy majesties! see where runs down
the yielding hollow of the Wounded Crown—

how named else? since on either side the cleft
what throned perfections! on the awful left
the queen Morgause of Orkney, on the right
Guinevere: O living breasts of love and light.
whom darkness shadows and an evil fate
making beyond their purpose the estate
of Camelot high-disastrous, yet not vain—
for lo, beneath, the Mystery of Helayne.
Nay now, my soul, be shy and very still;
nay now, and yet, my song, profess thy will
needs must proceed; nay, bid her pause not so:
doth she not image everywhere below
the truth of God in his own heaven?—then dare
even for a moment still to linger there.
This is the destined and thrice holy place
where is the Action and the last embrace,
this is the Mother of the Achievement, here
the Symbol that is fashioned everywhere
is passionate, mortal, and familiar: on—
alas, the Secret glowed and it is gone;
give back, but yet behold how on each side
the Champions in a veiled epiphany ride,
the left thigh Bors, the right is Percivale—
yea, I myself a guardian of the Grail.

But the Achievement issues from the mind—
and the pure brow the true thought lies behind,
is not this Lancelot? are not those deep eyes
Merlin, most cunning in his prophecies,

to whom the Quest by many a rune is known?
and O what name but Taliessin's own
fits the sweet mouth that utters no harsh wrong,
poet and warrior, challenge mixed with song?
And in the shining topmost of the hair?
Surely the crown which is the King is there.

Lady, hath any beauty been forgot?
Where is the loveliness of Camelot?
O the round throat! where is the Law? O Fair,
is not that straight back made beyond compare
one with that law? as with the prince, our lord,
the prince Dom Galahad, the high prince, the Accord
in Unity, the Achievement, Lancelot's son,

thy holy heart of inquest is made one.
O born of holy spells, O nourished long
in a convent of White Nuns, O only strong
to sit in the Perilous Siege and there look up
to find thyself the Achievement and the Cup,
thine is the blood of transmutation; now
thou art the tale and all the tale is thou.

A little longer yet let fantasy
veil the true centre of true things to be,
with added laughter and invention: see,
is there not something for those feet to be?
May not those soles be named as were the palms
(so soft with litanies and strong with psalms)?
Yea, let the left be Tristram and the right
Palomides, these two being chief in might
but yet without the Table; whose tale flows
into a fresh recital if the toes
daintily armoured: hark then, Sir Safere,
Sir Meliot de Logris, Sir Bellangere,
Sir Ozanna le Cure Hardy, Sir Lavaine;
these to the left, and to the right again—
hear how awful cycle closes well—
Sir Ector de Maris and Sir Lionel,
Sir La Cote Mal Taile, Sir Sigramore,
Sir Lucan the Butler, and the tale is o'er.

Wilt thou be perfect? teach thine eyes to see,
in all, in each, what thus I marked in thee.

A SONG OF PALOMIDES

*The lord Palomides, having tamed the Blatant
Beast, comes to his christening on the day of the ap-
parition of Galahad the High Prince and the open-
ing of the Quest.*

The soul that tamed the Blatant Beast
  came softly into hall;
Merlin the Wizard, Dubric the priest,
  and the knights and champions all
hailed Palomides in his youth,
and all these things for sudden sooth
Taliessin, the king's poet, sealed,
ere the hurt of the Wounded King was healed.

The soul that loved Iseult so long
  came sweetly into hall;
Percivale the subtle, Bors the strong,
  and the knights and champions all
brought Palomides to his see,
and all these things in testimony
Taliessin, the king's poet, sealed,
ere the hurt of the Wounded King was healed.

The soul that was fain to be baptized
  came shyly into hall,

in whom was the high prince recognized
   by the knights and champions all,
and Lancelot seeing him was glad,
and the Saracen prince in Galahad
Taliessin, the king's poet, sealed,
ere the hurt of the Wounded King was healed.

Palomides sat in the Perilous Chair,
   while the trumpets sang in the hall;
the King and his glowing chivalry there,
   the knights and champions all,
were lost and found in Christ the truth,
and all these things for sudden sooth
Taliessin, the king's poet, sealed,
ere the hurt of the Wounded King was healed.

TALIESSIN'S SONG
OF A PRINCESS OF BYZANTION

After the departure of Galahad and the other quest-
ing knights, King Arthur asks the lord Taliessin the
singer what shall be the end of these things; who
answers him by speaking of the High Prince under
the image of a dead Byzantine royalty.

'How should I dare,' the King's high port said,
sitting above the wine and broken bread,
'how should I dare show forth in song the glad
mystery of the prince Dom Galahad,
or any of those great souls who now go hence?
after what vigil, war, and pestilence,
the Grail shall find their hearts and they the Grail?
O King, but let a lesser rhyme avail,
for in my youthful journeys being gone
to the flowering gardens of Byzantion
I found in the Emperor's house a maiden there,
porphyrogenital, virginal, very fair,
whom the saints loved, the poor, and I. Even then
it pleased God to assume her soul from men
into that heaven from which she took her name:
Caelia she was, celestial was her fame—
whom that my love might have a place to sing
I made a poem for her buying—
hear it then, Arthur, and believe that thus

hath the high prince Galahad gone out from us,
and thus, at the fulfilment of the Quest,
the elect soul enters surely into rest.

Before the gate of Paradise a flame
of spirit shone, and Michael sought its name.
Now there the virtue which upon the throne
sits of each soul, is cried; none names its own,
but a great chorus, soft and sweet as dawn
on hillsides—those without and, far withdrawn,

the Gods about the Centre—all proclaim
of each redeemed the bright eternal name.
Here all was still; no proclamation stole
through the enringèd circles of the Whole,
and Michael asked again—there was no sound;
impatient heaven trembled all around,
speechless. The Archangel with a wrathless frown
upon that shy and brilliant flame looked down,
saying, "Ye princes, must even gods be dumb?
What name is hers who hath so bravely come
thus far unto Beatitude? what power
is praised in her at this most holy hour?
Patience?" The angels breathed: "No Patience, lord,
though she endured the hurt of every sword,
and neither moaned nor shuddered from it". "Joy?"
"No, though all dark distress did she destroy,
within her and about her." "Courage then?"
"No, though, none braver wandered among men."
"Justice?" "Not Justice, though none saw or heard
an unjust deed in her, and unjust word."
"Modesty?" "'Twas her signal, not her name,
though she went all her life in holy shame
of undue praising." "Temperance?" "Neither so,
though never she did intemperate longing show."
"Liberty?" "Nay, lord, though her life long she
set her own soul and all her friendships free
in an indoctrinated singleness."
"Virginity?" "Elsewhere she could not press

up to these portals; virginal through and through,
she made in her degree the whole world new."
"Obedience?" "Nay, to God's sole service thralled,
therein she toiled but thereby was not called."
"Wisdom?" "She had, being merely human." "Strength?"
"She kept, and Fortitude, through all her length
of days, untitled." "Perseverance then?"
"Not though, new-born, she never looked agen
on her old ways and ancient longings back,
but kept the straitness of the single track."
"Honour?" "But that was given to her long since;
she kept it still, transmuted." Then the prince
doubtfully glanced, saying: "Each thousand years
before this gate a royal soul appears,
in whom the virtues are so mingled all,
so brought to fullness, so perpetual,
it is named merely Goodness. Even thus
hath this bright vigilance grown up to us?"
But all the heavens were silent, till around
a sense of mightier utterance did abound,
in them, yet more than they; and Michael heard
the judgement of the plenipotential Word.
"Goodness was known in her—but thereabove
We gave to her no name save only love;
except that when We chose that love to sign
We sought no virtue, howsoe'er divine,
no potency, no title; as by chance
We softly did a mortal word advance,

We drew a littleness from casual things
and gave it meaning as We gave her wings,
and gave her ardour as We gave it light—
and whether she or it makes either bright
is whether her humility or Our grace
shines supernatural now in her glad face
more than the other; this ye cannot know,
ye gods, but that We joy to have it so.
Her name is Love-in-Caelia; so believe,
and by that name adore her and receive."
Even as the Revelation sank to rest,
she stood, in perfect union manifest:
heaven opened from her; from her inmost soul
the Centre issued in the unchanging Whole;
Michael himself in his young fellow saw
excelling Godhead in exceeding awe;
each than herself less glowing and less shy
the angels gazed, and softly a deep sigh
through the profundity of rapture fell:
"Praise to the Name Who doeth all things well.'"

THE SONG OF THE RIDING OF
GALAHAD

Though I be great in fame
who hath called me by name?
though I sit at the Table Round
who hath seen me or found?
what bishop or king or knight
hath spoken of me right?
though I be greatly styled
the Champion, the Merciful Childe,
the high priest Dom Galahad,
ye most shall they be glad
that none have at all forgot
I am also Lancelot.

I am no faery's son,
no ghostly myrmidon
loosed from the thick profound
shadows of underground
wherein Apollyon roars,
nor cherub from the doors
of heavenly beauty sent
to herald God's advent;
nor elemental knight
made human but to sight:
I am all man, I wot,
and born of Lancelot.

Ninth am I in degree
from Joseph of Arimathee:
bring sprung from holy men—
King Nappus, King Nacien,
the good King Helias,
King Lisais, King Jhonas
who rode in the land of Gaul,
King Launcelot, wisest of all,
King Ban, the last of the kings:
from whom in the eighth house springs
that knight whose peer is not,
my lord Sir Lancelot.

For my lord Sir Lancelot
in a marvel me begot
on my mother the Lady Helayne,

whom our fair Christ did ordain
for a covering and a shrine
to the body that is mine;
from his joy and agony
then I began to be;
his love being a fair thing
had holy assoiling
by the heavens' counsel and plot;
I also am Lancelot.

For the wise woman Briseis, she
who is kin to Nimue,
the Lady of the Lake,
did such enchantments make
that earth's best knight was stayed
on the heart of a pure maid,
and yet did nowise part
from his most passionate heart
and the image of Guinevere;
O miracle without peer
wherein I was begot,
who also am Lancelot.

For a length of seven suns
in a convent of White Nuns
where time grows mystical
 I watched the ritual
that compasses the design,
and into the burning wine

the star of Nowell hurled;
now is that time to the world
as thrice seven years; to God
beginning and period
are all at once, I wot,
and I am Lancelot.

Then on a festival
I sat in King Arthur's hall;
As Merlin sang, it befell—
I sat in the Perilous Sell
and all in a shining veil
over them went the Grail;
then each who looked to see
saw his own face in me.
I was for high and low
and the great King also
the vision that none forgot;
yea, and to Lancelot.

Though the Table's oath be vain
in the oath of Sir Gawaine,
who hath turned the world amiss
for the death of Sir Gaheris,
and brought the strength of his kin
a vengeance for blood to win
against the King's delight;
till Arthur march with his might
against the life of his friend,

these things shall have an end;
though the wood of the Table rot,
I also am Lancelot.

Where the king's army hard
presseth round Joyous Guard
and Lancelot moaneth amain
for the passion of his pain
that the King's wrath should prove
the evil frenzy of love,
and out of their hearts' dark sky
the many arrows fly
and the great catapults fling
their stones against knight and King,
let it not be forgot
I also am Lancelot.

Logres and Camelot
henceforth shall know me not;
nor the halls of the King's high towns
where the knights sit in their gowns,
when the tourney is done, at talk,
or clerks in the cloisters walk
speaking of mysteries,
and Easter that is our ease,
of Christ's incanacy
and the Holy Trinity;
yet far though I ride I wot
I also am Lancelot.

Though I be rarely styled,
the Champion, the Merciful Childe,
the high prince Dom Galahad,
not for that am I glad,
but now I am made most bold
to ride to King Pelleas' hold
where is a wound to heal;
thereafter I shall but kneel
where in a heavenly tongue
the final Mass is sung,
nor there shall it be forgot
I also am Lancelot.